WITHDRAWN

W9-CPC-198

TECH INDUSTRY

HIGH-TECH INDUSTRIAL SCIENCE

PAULA JOHANSON

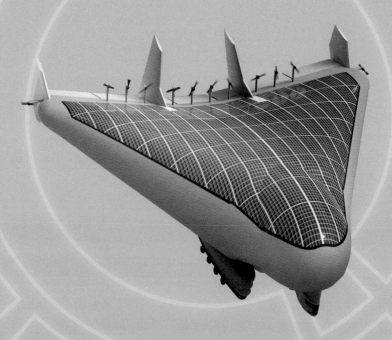

CRABTREE
Publishing Company

www.crabtreebooks.com

TECHNO PLANET

Author: Paula Johanson

Editors: Sarah Eason, John Andrews, and Petrice Custance

Proofreader and indexer: Wendy Scavuzzo

Editorial director: Kathy Middleton

Design: Paul Myerscough, Paul Oakley, and Jane McKenna

Cover design: Paul Myerscough

Photo research: Rachel Blount

**Production coordinator and
Prepress technician:** Margaret Amy Salter

Print coordinator: Margaret Amy Salter

Consultant: David Hawksett

Produced for Crabtree Publising Company by Calcium Creative.

Photo Credits:

t=Top, b=Bottom, br=Bottom Right, bl=Bottom Left,
bc=Bottom Center, r=Right, l=Left

CASE IH: 12–13; Sandvik: 15, 15l; Shutterstock: Alphaspirit: 23r;
Asharkyu: 6; Chesky: 27t; Cyo bo: 24; Ryan Fletcher: 28br; Huseyinbas:
11b; Praphan Jampala: 4; Matej Kastelic: 18; Andrei Kholmov: 5;
Alexander Kirch: 19; Kjpargeter: 29b; Lexaarts: 22–23; Ludinko: 19l;
Slavoljub Pantelic: 9t; Sean Pavone: 10–11; Pio3: 20–21; PokkO: 20r;
Science photo: 17; Peter Sobolev: 26b; Toa55: 16; VladSV: 8–9; Solar Ship
Inc.: 1, 24–25; Wikimedia Commons: Morio: 28t; Mrdeluna: 26–27; NASA:
7; Clem Rutter, Rochester, Kent: 28bl; Vanillase: 29b; Victorgrigas: 28bc.

Cover: Shutterstock: Slavoljub Pantelic, (right); PokkO, (bkgd)

Library and Archives Canada Cataloguing in Publication

Johanson, Paula, 1961-, author
        Tech industry / Paula Johanson.

(Techno planet)
Includes index.
Issued in print and electronic formats.
ISBN 978-0-7787-3604-2 (hardcover).--
ISBN 978-0-7787-3618-9 (softcover).--
ISBN 978-1-4271-1992-6 (HTML)

        1. Industries--Technological innovations--Juvenile literature.
2. Industries--Technological innovations--Social aspects--Juvenile
literature. 3. Industries--Technological innovations--Economic aspects--
Juvenile literature. I. Title.

HD45.J64 2017   j338'.064   C2017-903599-1
                                                    C2017-903600-9

Library of Congress Cataloging-in-Publication Data

CIP available at the Library of Congress

Crabtree Publishing Company
www.crabtreebooks.com   1-800-387-7650

Printed in Canada/092017/PB20170719

**Published in Canada
Crabtree Publishing**
616 Welland Ave.
St. Catharines, Ontario
L2M 5V6

**Published in the United States
Crabtree Publishing**
PMB 59051
350 Fifth Avenue, 59th Floor
New York, New York 10118

**Published in the United Kingdom
Crabtree Publishing**
Maritime House
Basin Road North, Hove
BN41 1WR

**Published in Australia
Crabtree Publishing**
3 Charles Street
Coburg North
VIC, 3058

CONTENTS

TECHNOLOGY AND INDUSTRY

Technology is an important part of industry. Tech innovations today, such as robots, satellites, and artificial intelligence, are as big as changes that happened during the Industrial Revolution that began around 200 years ago. In the Industrial Revolution, machines were invented that could do the work of ten people—even 100. New changes today, many using computers, help people do new kinds of work and share it around the world. Tech changes also mean that robots and other machines can now take over more and more work done by humans.

In hot and dangerous factories, workers can use remote-controlled robotic arms called "waldoes."

TECH AND THE WORKFORCE

The technology industry is a fast-growing one in North America. There are over 492,000 technology companies in the United States and about 71,000 in Canada. A whopping seven million people in the United States and about 864,000 people in Canada are employed in jobs that use or deal with technology. That is 4 percent of all jobs in the United States and 5.6 percent in Canada. Among those tech workers are people working in offices, in factories, and in the field. They have all kinds of industrial machines to help.

ROBOT CHALLENGES

People have always been concerned about using robots and tech to replace human workers. Some workers worry that robots and other machines will take their jobs. Others worry about robots becoming smarter than humans. However, some very dangerous jobs, such as mining deep underground or defusing bombs, are best done by machines. Sending people to Mars is too dangerous at the moment, so the Curiosity rover is exploring the planet's surface. Also, technology can do work that is boring and tiring.

A robot is more likely to be something like a forklift with a camera and a computer than the fancy androids in science fiction movies. Industrial robots are made to do a few tasks, not to be people. The science fiction writer Isaac Asimov imagined "Three Laws of Robotics." These laws said a robot could not harm a human, must follow orders, and must protect itself. That would be a good start for any future tech!

Mechanical arms make the same movements over and over to do the simplest jobs on assembly lines.

5

MAKING THINGS

Factories have been around for at least 200 years. In the past, they relied on machinery made with heavy materials such as iron and steel. Now, there are new tough but lightweight and highly adaptable materials, such as graphene. Special metal **alloys** work better than traditional metals. They are lighter and do not rust. New strong, durable, and easily recycled plastics can replace many metal parts. That saves both money and energy.

SMARTER ROBOTS

New robot assistants use software to learn how to find items and identify them. They learn from experience. Miso Robotics has developed Flippy, a burger-flipping robot. Flippy is already used in a chain of burger restaurants in California. Like a human, Flippy can learn from its mistakes. Even so, burger bots cannot do everything—yet. Human hands still have to deliver the burger to the customer. Where robots work alongside regular workers, this is called "cobotics."

Want to make a model of your own invention? There might be a 3-D printer at your town's library.

PRINTING PRODUCTS

In the past, big machines have been needed to make factory products. **Three-dimensional (3-D)** printing is changing the way things are made. A 3-D printer takes an image from a computer and turns it into a plastic object. Inventors can use 3-D printing to produce and test **prototypes**, or early versions of a product. When a 3-D printer can make objects right on-site, there is no need for production lines and stores of supplies.

Industrial designers can now see and test a product using computer graphics laid onto the real product. This is called **augmented reality (AR)**. It allows you to see your product from every angle, even from the inside. You learn how it connects to other products. That way, you can make sure the product is working well and efficiently. Put on a pair of Microsoft HoloLens goggles and you can even interact with **holograms** of your design or product. Microsoft calls this "mixed reality."

Many products are built in a truly "connected factory" that links together all aspects of how things are made and distributed. Thousands of **sensors** in factory equipment send information to computers that can figure out whether something is being built efficiently. Products fitted with sensors can then be followed on computers as they make their journey to a local store or anywhere in the world. This connection is called the "Internet of things."

The astronaut Scott Kelly wears a pair of Microsoft HoloLens goggles in a laboratory on the International Space Station (ISS).

7

DISTRIBUTING GOODS

Once products are made, they need to be shipped. For a long time, this has meant loading goods onto trucks, trains, and planes. However, new technology is finding ways to make distribution faster, safer, and more efficient.

PACKING AND POSTING

Smart warehouses do more than watch for temperature changes. Some have computerized networks of conveyors and elevators. Items for packaging come to the worker, rather than the worker looking for the items. Other warehouses have automated robot arms to pack goods into boxes. And the tech does not stop there. Food, drink, and medicines need special protection. Smart sensors inside food, drink, and medicine packaging can record and send information about moisture, temperature, and the amount of oxygen. This alerts suppliers to any problems with the products while they are shipped.

DELIVERING A BETTER ENVIRONMENT

Moving goods in a truck, train, or plane burns **fossil fuels** and creates **greenhouse gases**. All that carbon dioxide gas is helping cause climate change. There are many ways delivery services can now decrease their **carbon footprint**. One solution is to use small flying drones. Some electric drones can recharge on solar power. In London and New York City, little robots roll along sidewalks delivering restaurant food orders.

Cell phone apps such as Flex and PiggyBee are also helping the environment by using **crowdsourcing** for product delivery. Shippers can find ordinary travelers who are already heading to destinations near their customers to deliver goods for them.

For big deliveries, there are even bigger ideas. In 2017, a railway freight service opened between China and the United Kingdom. It carries boxcar shipments 7,500 miles (12,070 km) across Asia and Europe. Boxcar containers are also shipped across the oceans. Triple-E container ships are giant, low-emission vessels that carry 18,000 20-foot (6-m) long containers. These huge ships travel 114 miles (184 km) on 1 **kilowatt-hour** of energy per ton of cargo. That is much more energy-efficient than a jumbo jet, which moves a ton of cargo only 0.3 miles (0.5 km) on 1 kilowatt-hour of energy. Each ship also recycles the heat it produces. This saves up to 10 percent of its main engine power. That could be enough to power around 5,000 homes!

Sometimes a small electric drone is just the right size to deliver small packages over short distances.

Sometimes bigger is better! A Triple-E container ship is more fuel-efficient than a fleet of jumbo jets.

MAERSK LINE

SELLING AND BUYING

New technology has created many new ways to advertise products. Some print ads allow you to see a hologram video of a product. QR, or quick response, codes printed on ads can be read by smartphones to take a customer to a website. Instead of billboards, giant digital screens use LED lights for energy efficiency. In London's Piccadilly Circus and New York City's Times Square, the newest screens can even stream live video.

ADVERTISING GETS PERSONAL

Marketing goods or services online is more and more high tech. It is not just about showing the same ads to everyone who views a website. Digital marketing uses Internet filters to target a customer's interests. If a person searches online for information on steak, ads will be displayed about beef recipes and restaurants. On social media, ads will show vacations if the viewer has just come from a travel magazine's website.

Digital marketing is also creating content that loads extremely quickly on mobile devices. Google has developed an **open-source** format called Accelerated Mobile Pages (AMP). Websites and ads published in AMP format load almost instantly, even with videos.

Stores have new tech, too. They place small **transmitters**, called "beacons," around a store. Employees or automated systems can then send messages to customers' smartphones via Bluetooth. These messages can announce discounts or specials. In smart fitting rooms, customers can use their phones to change the lighting or to ask for different sizes or colors. A small computer chip called an RFID (radio-frequency identification) can be attached to most items in a store. Scanning RFID tags gives stores up-to-the-second information about their goods.

Giant digital LED screens bring color and advertising impact to Times Square.

10

Some stores you use may soon have no employees working at checkout counters. Customers are expected to walk in, pick up items they want to buy, and walk out. They still pay for what they buy! To get in or out, customers walk past a scanner at the door. Items are scanned, and the customer's credit card is charged automatically. This could help stop shoplifting. It could also save money by not having to pay sales clerks. However, what would customers do if they wanted help? What would you think of this tech if you worked in a store?

RFID tags can be used to keep track of products on their journey to a store and inside a store.

FARMING AND FOOD

No industry is more important than farming. Without farming, our grocery stores would be empty. New tech is making farming more efficient and our food safer. Tech is also making farming better for the environment.

TECH TAKES ON THE LAND

Electronic sensors are used in greenhouses and fields to test crops for diseases. Laser scanners can create 3-D images of fields so farmers can see how their crops are growing. High-tech sprinklers use data from satellites to decide how much water a field might need. There are even tractors being developed by companies such as Case IH and New Holland that work without a driver!

Farm managers use satellite pictures and **GPS** tracking to monitor crops and weather patterns. On some large farms, drones fly over fields to find diseased crops and the best place to target **pesticides**. Farmers track livestock and the growth of crops with RFID computer chips. Some food products use RFID or QR codes to allow consumers to follow the path of their food from farm to plate.

CHANGING FOOD

Much of our food contains extra chemicals that help keep it fresh and improve its texture or appearance. However, these chemicals can change the taste or look of the food. A new way to preserve food is to use water to apply high pressure to food. The food is put inside a strong plastic container and placed in a machine filled with water. A pump then raises the pressure of the water, which kills bacteria without affecting the food or its taste.

There are also companies that create **genetically modified** organisms (GMOs) by altering their **DNA**. The companies claim that GMOs can be used to produce crops that are less affected by insects and other pests. However, some scientists worry about the safety of GMOs and how they might harm the environment.

MAGIC FOOD

Changing how food looks and feels can be fun! A new invention, the Foodini, is a 3-D printer that can "print" food out of basic natural ingredients, such as dough, sauces, and meat. The ingredients are added to a plastic container, called a capsule, which is placed inside the printing machine. Then, as if by magic, your pizza, pretzel, or ravioli is ready to be cooked!

TECHNO PLANET

Some farm equipment is being made easier to control with small hand movements or by using computers. Tractors fitted with GPS systems can work automatically, saving time and physical effort. Farmers no longer have to be tall and strong to operate machines! These changes allow farmers who are aging or disabled to harvest a field or load a truck with grain.

The newest tractors need human programmers, but they can plow and harvest without a driver!

DRILLING, DIGGING, AND MINING

Essential metals such as iron and copper are taken from the ground and used to make many things. The oil and gas needed to power our homes, factories, and transportation also come from the ground. We rely on the industries that drill, dig, and mine to find these materials. New technologies help those industries find what they need. For example, Harrier Aerial Surveys in Canada flies drones over miles of rough ground to find and examine promising sites for mining companies.

FINDING OIL AND GAS

New oil drilling technologies can get more oil or natural gas out of a well. Steam injection pushes steam into wells to force oil toward the surface or to make the oil less thick so it is easier to extract. Water injected into an oil well can contain added **nutrients** that wake up organisms in the ground. Those organisms then break down the oil into a form that is easier to extract.

Large amounts of oil and gas are trapped in rocks far underground. Fracking is a technology that releases that oil and gas. It forces water mixed with chemicals deep into the ground to break up, or fracture, rocks. New fracking techniques have been developed. "Zipper fracking" uses two wells drilled side by side to crack rocks more deeply and produce more oil or gas.

Many people worry about fracking and other technologies for extracting fossil fuels. Fracking can cause earth tremors. Some fracking chemicals and gases get into streams or even wells used for drinking water.

SAVING LIVES

Mining work can be dangerous. New technology could help prevent injuries—and even save lives. Remote-control mining machinery and robot mining tools keep people away from dangerous areas. Sensors in mine workers' clothing can track

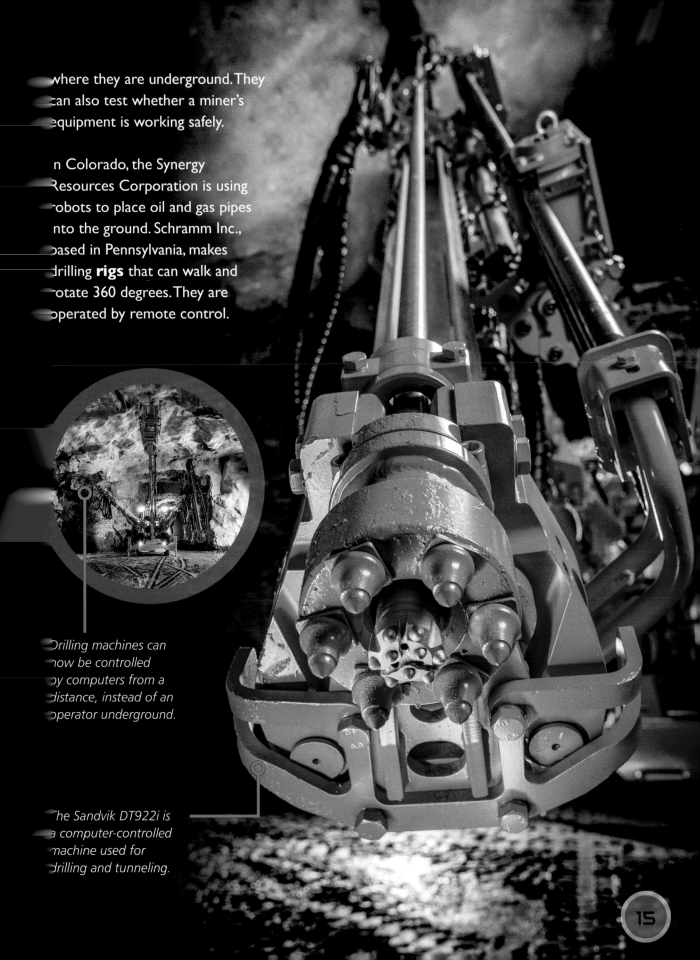

where they are underground. They can also test whether a miner's equipment is working safely.

In Colorado, the Synergy Resources Corporation is using robots to place oil and gas pipes into the ground. Schramm Inc., based in Pennsylvania, makes drilling **rigs** that can walk and rotate 360 degrees. They are operated by remote control.

Drilling machines can now be controlled by computers from a distance, instead of an operator underground.

The Sandvik DT922i is a computer-controlled machine used for drilling and tunneling.

FEEL THE POWER!

There is only so much oil, gas, and coal that we can get from the ground or the ocean floor. In time, we will run out of all of these resources. We must have electricity and other kinds of power for our homes and businesses. New technology is vital for finding new ways to create or store that power.

KEEPING IT CLEAN

Most of our energy currently comes from big power stations. **Hydroelectric** power stations create energy through the flow of water, so they are cleaner, or release less greenhouse gases, than stations that burn oil, coal, or gas. Nuclear power is energy produced by splitting **atoms**. It is also a clean method of producing energy, and plants can work for many years. Because this form contains dangerous **radiation**, nuclear power stations must follow strict building and safety codes. There is controversy about using nuclear power because of accidents in the past, at power plants in the United States, Ukraine, and Japan. However, nuclear tech can also save lives. Radiation is used in hospitals to help treat cancer and other diseases.

Some spacecraft use nuclear power, such as the New Horizons space probe. Powered by its own small nuclear power plant, it passed the dwarf planet Pluto in 2015 and is traveling beyond our solar system. The same technology could be used to build smaller, cheaper, and safer power plants in towns and cities on Earth. They could even be built under ground or under water, where they would be even safer.

These water tubes are used for growing **algae**. *It will be harvested to make oil to burn for fuel.*

ENDLESS SUPPLIES

The cleanest power of all comes from renewable sources. Renewable sources of power, such as the sun and the sea, will never run out. These sources of power are considered clean because they do not release greenhouse gases. Engines called **turbines** are used to create wind power and wave power, and solar panels are used to capture sunlight and create electricity. Small hydroelectric turbines built on rivers or streams allow a single home or small settlement to create electricity on the spot.

Even plants can produce energy. Their oils make good **biofuel**. This is used mostly in cars and trucks. It can also be used to power pumps and make electricity. Biofuel is even being made from the waste gases of fossil fuel extraction. An oil refinery in Alberta uses algae to make biofuel by recycling carbon dioxide from the oil drilling process.

Once a solar panel or wind farm is built, it can work for years making electric power.

ENERGY EFFICIENCY

Sometimes the answer is not more power, but a more efficient way to use it. Energy efficiency saves money and natural resources, such as gas, oil, and water. It can also cut down on greenhouse gases. Technology plays an important part in finding new, smart ways to save energy.

AT HOME AND WORK

Homes, offices, and industries all use energy for light, heating, and cooling. They also use energy to power machinery, from fridges to factory production lines. Wireless sensors inside devices can link to the Internet and send real-time information about temperature, humidity, and other things that affect energy use. Changes can then be made to save energy. In industrial plants, all this information can be monitored on computer systems, so the plant works as efficiently as possible.

An energy-efficient building can be a comfortable place to live or work.

Lighting eats up a lot of energy. In the workplaces of the United States, lighting uses more than 10 percent of all electricity. Smart lighting tech uses sensors to monitor daylight and the movement of people. If there is no one in the building, why keep the lights on? The latest low-power LED lighting uses around 75 percent less energy and lasts about 25 times longer than old-style lightbulbs. And how about windows that automatically change shading as the light changes? Sensor and **microprocessor** tech now make this happen.

Insulation is the easiest answer for keeping buildings warm in winter and cool in summer. The newest foam insulation panels use materials that are lighter, more energy-efficient, and less likely to catch fire. Sometimes new tech means finding new ways to use old-fashioned materials. Sheep's wool is now used as fire-resistant, noise-absorbing insulation in attics and walls. It is renewable and very energy efficient.

HEAT AND POWER

One of the smartest ways to use energy efficiently is to produce heat and power at the same time. The latest CHP (combined heat and power) plants link a boiler to a turbine. This can save industries 20 percent on their energy costs. It can also cut carbon emissions by up to 30 percent. Companies such as EnerTwin in the Netherlands make small-scale CHP plants. They provide electricity and heat for hot water in homes and small businesses. These efficient boilers have fewer emissions than an ordinary home furnace.

Want to turn on your porch light at home while you are away? Or save energy by turning down the heat? There are apps for that.

LED lightbulbs are a practical, energy-efficient choice. They use less electricity than other bulbs, are cooler, and last much longer.

09:34am smartHome

HOME AUTOMATION

DEVICE   STATUS   TO DO
BACKYARD   RECORDING..   VIEW
CAMERA

14

SMART BUILDINGS

We live, work, and go to school in buildings. They need to be efficient enough to do their job. There have been many new developments in design and materials for construction. Buildings now are connected to the Internet and can be monitored on computers. Some buildings can even create their own energy and help clean the air.

MAKING BUILDINGS

Technology is helping create new construction materials. Most plastics are made from petroleum. Bioplastics are made from renewable sources such as corn flour and even recycled plastic. Newlight Technologies, a company in California, makes bioplastic using waste carbon emissions. Liquid wood is a bioplastic invented by a German company, Tecnaro. It is made from paper industry waste products. Liquid wood looks like wood, but can be used in the same ways as plastic.

These amazing "supertrees" in Singapore's Gardens by the Bay complex make their own clean energy.

An amazing new material is self-healing concrete. When the concrete is poured, small capsules are added. The capsules hold bacteria that can make limestone. If the concrete cracks and water seeps in, the capsules dissolve. The bacteria then make limestone, which seals the cracks. This self-healing concrete can even be sprayed on the outside of existing buildings.

And how about a house that can be printed on a 3-D printer in 24 hours! In 2016, the Apis Cor company did exactly that in Russia. The printer "ink" was a concrete mix. The house cost just over $10,000 to build. It should last up to 175 years.

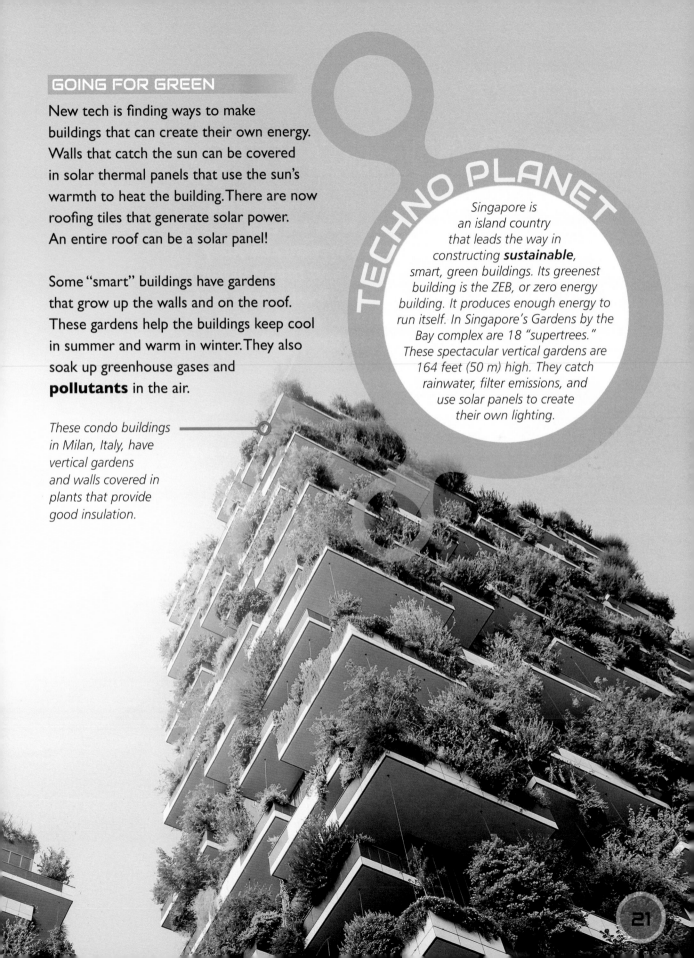

GOING FOR GREEN

New tech is finding ways to make buildings that can create their own energy. Walls that catch the sun can be covered in solar thermal panels that use the sun's warmth to heat the building. There are now roofing tiles that generate solar power. An entire roof can be a solar panel!

Some "smart" buildings have gardens that grow up the walls and on the roof. These gardens help the buildings keep cool in summer and warm in winter. They also soak up greenhouse gases and **pollutants** in the air.

These condo buildings in Milan, Italy, have vertical gardens and walls covered in plants that provide good insulation.

TECHNO PLANET

*Singapore is an island country that leads the way in constructing **sustainable**, smart, green buildings. Its greenest building is the ZEB, or zero energy building. It produces enough energy to run itself. In Singapore's Gardens by the Bay complex are 18 "supertrees." These spectacular vertical gardens are 164 feet (50 m) high. They catch rainwater, filter emissions, and use solar panels to create their own lighting.*

MASS COMMUNICATION

It might seem strange, but e-mail and texting were once seen as high-tech. Now we can communicate with each other instantaneously through smartphones, tablets, and many other kinds of computerized digital devices. Businesses and industries use the latest communication tech to talk to their suppliers, one another, and us.

COMPLETE CONNECTION

Modern communications technology relies on hundreds of satellites in orbit around Earth. When you use your smartphone, watch TV, or listen to the radio, you are often using satellites. Communications also rely on ultra-fast broadband Internet. The Internet uses satellites but also thousands of miles of copper wire and **fiber-optic cables**.

This tech allows businesses to use powerful computers and programs to collect information, or data. Everyone's online behavior, such as Internet searches and social media activity, creates data about their interests and habits. That data is sometimes sold to businesses who read that data to figure out what products or services people may be interested in so they can advertise effectively.

Some new ways of communicating come from surprising places. Those LED lights above your head can also send data to your computer. They do it so quickly that you cannot see it happening. It may not be long before we talk about Li-Fi as much as Wi-Fi.

MARCH OF THE BOTS

In Montreal, Alan Emtage created the first Internet search engine in 1990. The McGill University student called his search tool "Archie." It is a kind of robot, but one made of computer code instead of wires and metal. A computer program on a website that makes automatic actions can be called a robot, or bot. Bots do repetitive tasks automatically, at speeds much faster than any human. Some are useful tools for research. Some bots in online social networks can influence people's opinions. They can also steal personal information. This is called **identity theft**.

TOO MUCH COMMUNICATION?

In the United States alone, people look at their smartphones more than 9 billion times a day. With all this communication, there are concerns for privacy. Pretty Good Privacy (PGP) encryption increases the security of e-mail messages. PGP is a way to authenticate data from a trusted source. It is also used for encrypting large files and for signing contracts. How safe do you feel when you go online?

Fiber-optic cables carry many phone calls or Internet connections at once in tiny flickers of light.

Some communications satellites carry TV signals. Others keep cell phones connected.

GET MOVING!

Transportation is an essential part of our lives. Industry and business need to move goods and people around quickly and efficiently. Technology has already given us cars, trucks, planes, and trains. Now, new technologies are revolutionizing the many ways we travel.

LOOKING UP

More and more people are flying, for both pleasure and business. New, super-size airliners carry more people than ever before. The Airbus 380-800 is the world's largest passenger plane. It is 238 feet 8 inches (72.7 m) long and can carry up to 853 passengers on two decks. Emissions are low, and around 25 percent of the plane is made of carbon-fiber reinforced plastic, so the plane is lighter and more fuel efficient.

Planes burn a lot of fuel and create greenhouse gases. Solar-powered planes are being developed to carry cargo or passengers, with no refueling stops. The Solar Ship is a new Canadian airship. It can be powered by solar panels spread across the top of its wings. The Solar Ship can carry goods to remote areas that have no roads or railroads.

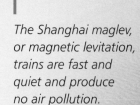

The Shanghai maglev, or magnetic levitation, trains are fast and quiet and produce no air pollution.

ON THE ROAD

Electric vehicles are on the increase. The latest technology means that batteries can charge in seconds and last for hundreds of miles. The Tesla Gigafactory in the Nevada desert aims to produce battery cells for up to 1 million electric vehicles by 2020. The factory will have the biggest floor area of any building in the world. It will also generate all its own power from solar panels covering the whole roof and in the surrounding hills.

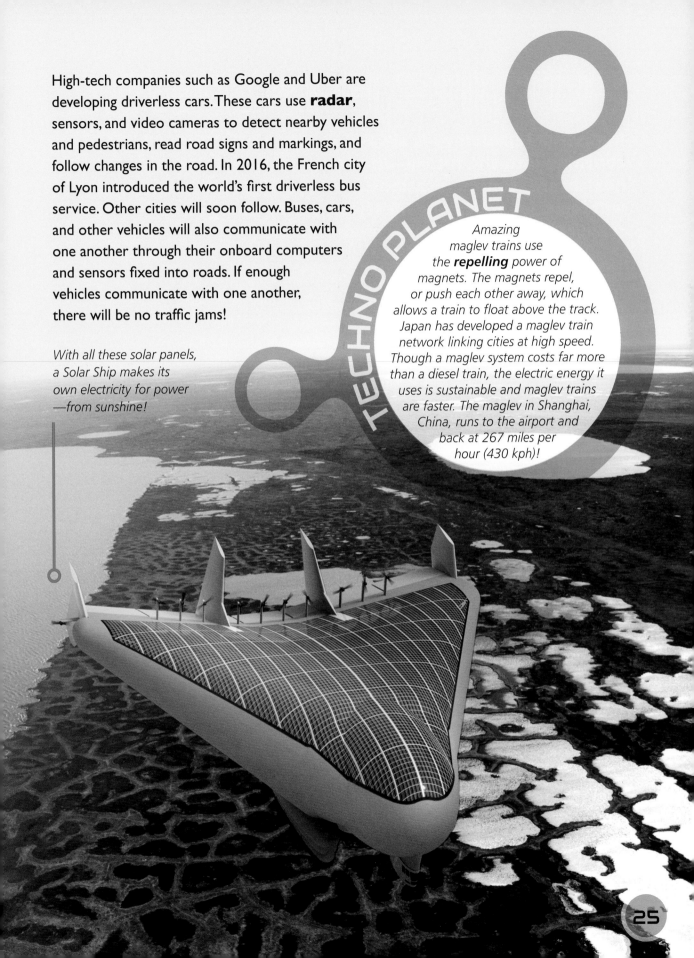

High-tech companies such as Google and Uber are developing driverless cars. These cars use **radar**, sensors, and video cameras to detect nearby vehicles and pedestrians, read road signs and markings, and follow changes in the road. In 2016, the French city of Lyon introduced the world's first driverless bus service. Other cities will soon follow. Buses, cars, and other vehicles will also communicate with one another through their onboard computers and sensors fixed into roads. If enough vehicles communicate with one another, there will be no traffic jams!

With all these solar panels, a Solar Ship makes its own electricity for power —from sunshine!

TECHNO PLANET

*Amazing maglev trains use the **repelling** power of magnets. The magnets repel, or push each other away, which allows a train to float above the track. Japan has developed a maglev train network linking cities at high speed. Though a maglev system costs far more than a diesel train, the electric energy it uses is sustainable and maglev trains are faster. The maglev in Shanghai, China, runs to the airport and back at 267 miles per hour (430 kph)!*

FUTURE FANTASTIC

Industrial technology is always on the move. This will continue into the future—in transportation, factories, healthcare, communications… everything! New tech will focus on improving lifestyles, saving energy and resources, and helping our environment.

KEEPING TRACK

Drones are already delivering goods to people. In the future, warehouses might take to the air, too, carrying lightweight products or medical supplies. Public transit might include small urban transport pods for just two or three persons. In California, the SpaceX company is working on the Hyperloop passenger and freight system. This quiet and energy-efficient transportation could push a large pod through an almost airless tube at speeds of more than 700 miles per hour (1,127 kph). There are already driverless trains, buses, and cars. Soon it could be a computer, not a pilot, flying you to your destination.

WHERE ARE ROBOTS GOING?

No one is sure what the future holds for robots. Supermarkets might have robot delivery systems that bring goods out of warehouses right to your home. In hospitals, robots might be programmed to do routine surgery. If you cannot travel to an event or meeting, why not use a telepresence robot to take your place? Just log in, and the robot acts for you. Robots do not have to be life-size. Microbots are tiny robots that could work together, like ants, to fix problems in small spaces. They could even team up to assemble buildings or industrial products.

Telepresence robots can carry people's faces and voices into the office or classroom.

BACK TO NATURE

Future tech will not always be high-tech. The science of synthetic biology combines the power of natural living cells with the power of engineering technology. This could create sensors that test land and water for pollutants. Waste could be identified for use as biofuel. Crop quality and yields could be improved. This kind of technology will particularly help people in poor countries. It is exciting to think that, in the future, technology will improve the lives of so many people around the world!

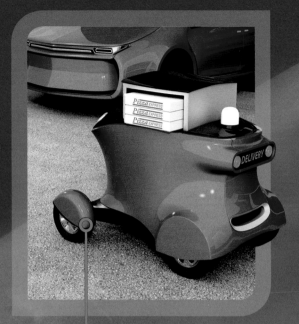

Tiny rolling drones will be big enough to deliver small packages short distances.

Waterloop designed this streamlined entry in SpaceX's Hyperloop pod design competition.

Waterloop

TECH TIMELINE

1455
Johannes Gutenberg prints the Bible on a printing press with movable type

1837
First telegraph system is patented

1876
Alexander Graham Bell patents the telephone

1906
Canadian experimenter Reginald Fessenden sends the first voice and music radio signals

1769
James Watt **patents** the steam engine that powers the Industrial Revolution

1867
French gardener Joseph Monier patents his idea for reinforced concrete

1903
The Wright brothers make the first controlled airplane flight

1764
James Hargreaves invents the "spinning jenny," a machine for spinning large amounts of wool

1850s
Method for mass-producing steel is discovered

1886
Karl Benz patents the first car powered by an internal combustion engine

1820s
Charles Babbage starts to build the Difference Engine calculating machine—the forerunner of the computer

1913
Henry Ford introduces the assembly line to his factories

1937
Invention of the self-propelled combine harvester by the Massey-Harris company

1969
First link is made on the ARPANET networking system—the birth of the Internet

2007
Apple introduces the iPhone

1983
Chuck Hull invents the first 3-D printer

1943–46
J. Presper Eckert and John Mauchly construct ENIAC, the first modern computer

1971
Computer programmer Ray Tomlinson invents e-mail

1999
Research in Motion releases the first BlackBerry device

2017
First "robofarm" opens in Japan

1938
Discovery of nuclear fission paves the way for the nuclear age

1970s
First personal computers

1989
Tim Berners-Lee designs the World Wide Web

2009
Google launches its self-driving car project

1925
Scottish inventor John Logie Baird transmits a human face on TV

1962
Launch of Telstar, the first communications satellite

1973
Martin Cooper makes the first cell phone call

2000
Honda creates ASIMO, an advanced human-like robot

GLOSSARY

Please note: Some **bold-faced** words are defined where they appear in the book.

algae Simple plants that grow in water

alloys Metals made from two different metals or one metal and another material

atoms Tiny particles that make up materials

biofuel Fuel made of natural materials

carbon footprint The amount of carbon dioxide released into the atmosphere by the actions of a person or group

crowdsourcing Asking a large number of people for input for a project

DNA A substance that carries genetic information in the cells of plants and animals

fiber-optic cables Cables made of fibers of glass or plastic that transmit light

fossil fuels Fuel formed in the ground from the remains of plants or animals

genetically modified Organisms that have one or more of their genes changed

GPS Global positioning system—a way of navigating using satellites

greenhouse gases Gases such as carbon dioxide that warm the atmosphere

holograms Pictures that are produced by a laser and look three-dimensional

kilowatt-hour A measure of electrical energy that is equal to 1,000 watts of power for one hour

LED A kind of light that is very energy-efficient

microprocessor A device in a computer that manages information

nutrients Substances needed for something to grow and live

open-source Computer software with source code that can be used or changed by anyone

patents Obtains a legal paper that gives an inventor the sole rights over an invention

pesticides Chemicals used to kill insects and other pests on plants and crops

pollutants Substances that make land, air, and water dirty and unsafe

QR A barcode carrying information that can be read by a smartphone

radar A system that sends out pulses, which bounce off objects and come back

radiation Strong energy produced by nuclear power and can be dangerous

rigs Collections of machinery used for drilling

sensors Devices that can be placed in a body or an object to send information

sustainable Able to be used without being completely used up or destroyed

three-dimensional (3-D) A shape having or seeming to have the three dimensions of length, width, and height

transmitters Devices that send out radio or TV signals

turbines Engines with blades that are turned by water, steam, or air

LEARNING MORE

BOOKS

Faust, Daniel R. *Manufacturing Robots* (Robots and Robotics).
PowerKids Press, 2016.

Klinger, Allen. *Modern Digital Technology: From Ideas to Devices.*
World Scientific Publishing, 2017.

Sjonger, Rebecca. *Robotics Engineering and Our Automated World.*
Crabtree Publishing, 2017.

WEBSITES

www.nationalgeographic.com/science
Discover all kinds of fascinating science and technology stuff on
National Geographic's science website.

www.ic.gc.ca/eic/site/icgc.nsf/eng/home
The Innovation, Science and Economic Development Canada
website has information on many topics, including business,
industry, science, and technology.

www.nasa.gov/audience/foreducators/robotics/
home/ROVER.html#.VmbUA7TJt0I
Learn how to drive a Mars rover without draining all of its battery
power:

INDEX

About the Author

Paula Johanson is in the Graduate Certificate in Digital Humanities program at the University of Victoria, Canada. Her nonfiction credits include 34 books on science, health, and literature for educational publishers. Paula would like to dedicate this book to Ryan and Kevin, learning their family business: Computers… and Adventure!